WHY CAN'T I BRING MYSELF TO WORK?

Lynn Deanne Childress
Windsor, England
October 14, 2001

WHY CAN'T I BRING MYSELF TO WORK?

Lynn Deanne Childress

First published by AuthorHouse 06/01/04

ISBN: 1-4140-6528-0 (e-book)
ISBN: 1-4184-2629-6 (Paperback)

Library of Congress Control Number: 2004091431

This book is printed on acid free paper.

Printed in the United States of America
Bloomington, IN

To my family, new friends,
medical personnel, and public
employees
who showed me what can be
done by working together
And to a certain man, who first
asked me
"Have you ever thought about
coming back to America?"
and then continued to ask me,
again and again
"When are you coming home?"
Until I finally did
Thank-you

Contents

1.

Why can't I bring myself to work?

I came home to the small town that I had left at the age of 18, vowing at the time never to return. Only a few family members were left there to welcome me. I arrived with my son, who was American in name only, and two suitcases full of European clothes. Everything else had been left behind. We were 21st-century immigrants, but unlike earlier generations, we did not have a community of fellow immigrants to provide support and encouragement.

When I looked around, I saw classmates who had $350,000 homes and SUVs. Some of them had gone through a series of jobs, each with more status and more money. Others had become life-long elementary schoolteachers. A few fortunate ones were already retiring. But they all had one thing in common: they had worked. And for me, that was the road not taken.

By all normal standards, I was a failure. I had no job, no car, no house, no possessions, no friends, no husband, and no plan for my life. In fact, I was just one step away from life at the YMCA, if I could get in.

To make matters worse, I
had a doctorate from Oxford
University and the highest
possible score (800) on the
verbal portion of the Graduate
Record Exam.

I should have succeeded, yet
something had profoundly
gone wrong. The question was
"Why couldn't I bring myself
to work?"

2.

How do people cope with the necessity of working?

We are all in a state of collective denial.

In America, we hold the values of freedom and equality as supremely important. Nevertheless, the majority of Americans between the ages of 18 and 65 (or is it 75 these days?) spend most of their waking hours in the workplace. And there are few places that are less free, less democratic, and less egalitarian than the workplace.

Most people have little choice about whether to work and, once employed, little choice about whom they work with. Work is not something that we freely choose to do or not do. It is an involuntary activity, a necessity that we learn to cope with. What is the urge to own rental property or stock market shares, if not the desire to obtain income without participating in the workplace? Is not the dream of being rich really the desire to have enough money to buy your freedom from the workplace?

Deep down, if we face the truth, there is a part of us that would rather not work.

3.

What is the value of one hour of my time?

The value of one hour of my time is the same as that of every other human being.

Human life is precious. One hour in the life of a mentally disabled grocery store employee is not worth less than one hour in the life of a CEO. Nevertheless, the hourly rate of pay does not reflect this basic truth. The present economic system compensates people according to the monetary worth of what they produce in that hour—without regard to their worth as a human being.

Under such an economic system, valuable activities are defined as worthless: an hour of motherly love, an hour of conversation, an hour of prayer. Yet we know in our heart that we cannot live without these "worthless" things.

I would rather fall down upon the broken pavement than participate in such a morally corrupt economic system. Let us start from the premise of a worldwide *uniform hourly wage* and rebuild the world of work.

4.

How can I escape the trajectory of the past?

Start again, wherever you are at.

At age 18, there are infinite possibilities. We could go to any college, marry any person, pursue any career, live any place in the world. By the age of 50, we are educated in a certain subject, employed in a particular job, married to a specific person, and living in one place. Every decision that we have made in the intervening 32 years has eliminated certain possibilities from our life, leaving open a narrower range of options for moving forward. This is a normal and natural process. We can see the same thing happen in the life of a company, an organization, or a government.

When the noose of our circumstances tightens around our neck, we die and start again. And so too should this be the case for our institutions and social structures.

I left everything and returned to the place where I started from at age 18, in order to start again in a new direction.

At age 50, there are infinite possibilities, plus additional advantages.

The first advantage is that no one expects anything from you any more.   Your career fell short, your spouse and children were a disappointment, you earned less money than you hoped to, you did not achieve any lasting accomplishments. In short, the pressure to make the "right" choices to succeed is gone.

The second advantage is that you are less fearful. You do not need to choose a course of action that will guarantee security because you have already survived numerous downturns. In short, you know that you can take care of yourself.

The trajectory of the past always terminates wherever you are at. Start again.

5.

How am I damaged by working?

Work distorts our true value.

What we do for a living is the single most important source of our wealth, our identity, and our status in society. Our place in the workforce hierarchy defines where we (and our children) fit into the world in terms of income, status, authority, and the degree of respect accorded to us. The job that we take either impoverishes our self-worth or overinflates it—and therein lies the damage.

Work, as it is presently structured, makes us "less" or "more" than what we really are.

6.

Does work prevent me from achieving my purpose in life?

Work is not my purpose in life.

Many people equate their work with their purpose in life. Their job is the center of their entire existence. It is their reason for being. Twenty percent of the working population report that they have no close personal relationships outside of the workplace. And for a much higher percentage, work is the defining feature of their life.

Job loss or retirement for such individuals is life-threatening.

Others use their work as a means to accomplish their purpose in life. The money earned at a job is used to fund dreams or goals that are unrelated to the activity performed at work. For these individuals, there is typically an underlying discomfort with work. The time at work is time taken away from the purpose of their life. And yet, they see no alternative way of making their dream come true.

But for me, my purpose in life is the most important thing. Work prevents me

from achieving my purpose
in life because, for some us,
our purpose has no recognized
economic value in the current
historical circumstances.

My purpose in life is not
recognized as "work."

7.

How do I resist the pressure to work?

I follow my purpose in life.

The family is the main source of pressure to work. Parents force young people to leave home and become self-sufficient; income-producing adults divorce their jobless spouses; siblings refuse financial assistance to non-working brothers and sisters. In some cases, power within the extended family follows the same pattern as the outside world. Those without employment bring disgrace

to the family and may find
themselves marginalized or
ostracized. Family members
who are unable to integrate
themselves into the workforce
are viewed as irresponsible and
immature.

The state is a secondary source
of pressure. The government
provides minimal assistance
to those without work. This
assistance is temporary and
can only be received if you
participate in a job-finding
program.

Without income from work
and without assistance from
family or the state, the pressure
to provide the basic necessities

of life—food, shelter,
transportation, health care, and
clothing—is substantial. Most
people will work. If they work,
they consume, and the present
economic system is sustained.

By not working, I put pressure
on the socio-economic system.

8.

How can I live without material objects?

Learn to love nothingness.

Most of the houses that I have visited in the United States are unbelievably cluttered. Things are piled on the floor, the furniture, and every available surface. It is impossible to really clean these houses. The television is turned on. Typically, there will be a candle burning in a jar: the pleasant smell makes the visual and audio clutter bearable. I have never seen candles like these in Europe.

The problem of the "house" is misdefined. The house is too small for the family or too big to be looked after. One or more of the family members never pick up or put away. Everyone is too busy—with work, with activities, with the day to day necessities of life.

The *real* problem of the "house" is too many material things.

Always choose to have less rather than more.

9.

Why is learning to love nothingness important?

The desire for material objects is an admission of neediness.

Material objects are the evidence of our private, psychological neediness. They are the representations of our desires, our will, and the depth of our need, shamelessly exhibited for everyone to see.

The desire to own or possess certain things takes hold like a deep hunger. Work becomes the means to obtain the object of your desire. You do not

work for the pure joy of it,
but rather because you have
developed a dependency. The
power of the desire is so strong
that you are willing to debase
yourself—working long hours,
doing something you hate or
have no respect for, under
degrading conditions. No
matter how hard you try to deny
it, you are under the thumb of
material things.

By learning to love
nothingness, material objects
(and the owners of those
objects) no longer have any
power over you.

10.

Without work, what is my source of direction?

I follow my heart.

Relationships have always been the highest priority in my life. I have spent countless hours thinking about relationships— how to start them, how to nurture them, how to fix them when they get broken, how to fix myself when I am damaged by them, how to make them everlasting.

The direction of my life has been set by "love." Love shows me the path of my destiny. It is impossible for me to focus on work, when all of my being is consumed by love for another—someone to whom I am passionately devoted and willing to follow.

Love, not work, is the goal of my life.

11.

Why should I work?

We should work as an expression of our love for others.

Our deepest fulfillment is to work for the perfection, the happiness, and well-being of humanity. All those other people out there—kind, vulnerable, doing their best types—are worth working for. They are worth the sacrifice of our time and of our life.

It is true that the present structure of work is imperfect. Somehow we must find a way to compensate all forms of human effort, not just those efforts that produce material objects or the narrow range of monetarily recognized services.

But whatever work I do, if it brings happiness to someone else, if it meets someone's needs, if it saves someone's life, it is worth the sacrifice of my life.

My friends, I am off to find a job.

Keep your spirit unbroken.

*The unrealized dreams of our
generation may be fulfilled in yours.*

Let's talk about it

For those of you who would like to discuss this book as a small group (6-8 people), here is a plan of action.

Do one chapter per session, but omit chapter 1 (i.e. a total of 10 discussion sessions).

Have one person read the chapter out loud to the group.

Have each person say what word in the chapter stands out in their mind.

Have a second person read the chapter out loud to the group.

Have each person say what phrase stands out in their mind and why that particular phrase seems to jump out at them.

At this point, begin discussing the one or more of the further questions (see below).

To conclude your discussion session, have a third person read the entire chapter.

Have each person say what action (if any) they feel that they should take because of reading this chapter.

Those who choose non-action may wish to say why they

think that non-action is the best
course.

Further questions

2

- What is that part of you that would rather not work?

- Is the problem with work the fact that it takes up most of your waking hours?

- What choices do you have when it comes to work?

3

- What are some valuable activities that have no economic value?

- If you were paid the same amount of money for every hour of your time, no matter what you were doing, how would you spend your time?

4

- What prevents you from starting again?

- What possibilities have you eliminated from your life?

- What advantages would there be in starting over?

5

- In what way does your work make you less than what you really are?

- In what way does your work make you more than what you really are?

- Does retirement put an end to this type of damage?

6

- Do you have close personal relationships with people you do not work with either now or in the past? What does this mean for your life?

- What are some alternative ways to achieve your dreams or life goals?

- Does work enhance or impede your purpose in life?

7

- What are the pressures that force you to work?

- What would be the consequences if you resisted those pressures?

- What fears prevent you from resisting the pressures?

8

- What is the real problem of your house?

- Would having fewer things help to solve the problem?

- Would having more time help to solve the problem?

9

- What do you desire most in life?

- Do you work in order to attain this desire?

- How can you free yourself from the power of this desire?

10

- How has your life been defined by following your heart?

- If you were to allow the direction of your life to be set by what you love, where would you go?

11

- Does your work allow you to express your deepest self?

- What are your true motives for working?

Notes

Notes

About the Author

Lynn Deanne Childress completed
her doctorate in English Literature
at Oxford University, under the
supervision of Prof. John Bayley,
and after his retirement, Prof. Terry
Eagleton.

www.ingramcontent.com/pod-product-compliance
Lightning Source LLC
Chambersburg PA
CBHW020409290526
45785CB00005B/2485